©1998 by Sara De Luca. All rights reserved.
ISBN 0-9665478-0-2

Edited by Fred Burwell and Mary Hughes-Greer
Design and Layout by Jeremy Saperstein
Printed by BookMasters, Inc.
All photos courtesy of Sara De Luca.

Address all correspondence to:
Acorn Whistle Press
907 Brewster Avenue
Beloit WI 53511

First Edition

Songs From an Inland Sea

SARA DE LUCA

ACORN WHISTLE PRESS

I wish to thank my editors, Fred Burwell and Mary Hughes-Greer, poets and mentors John Caddy and Sandra Adelmund, and my husband, Michael De Luca, for his faithful and enthusiastic support of my work.

-Sara De Luca

Some of these poems have appeared previously, as follows:

"Balsam Beach" , *Mankato Poetry Review,* **and** *The MacGuffin.*

"Pickles", *Mankato Poetry Review.*

"Voyage", "Skating Near the Barn", and "Splicing the Rope", *Acorn Whistle.*

"Circle Skirt", *Array.*

"New Kittens" was included in the anthology *Between Two Waters.*

"The Coffee Train" and **"Real Estate"**, *Wolf Head Quarterly.*

"Nourishment" and **"Sunday Drive"**, *North Coast Review.*

"Grounding", *Fauquier Poetry Journal.*

"Threshing Day" was included in the anthology *This Old Tractor.*

"Whipped Cream On Sunday", *Lullwater Review.*

To my mother, who loved the rhythm of dairy farming

and to the memory of my father, who loved the music of nature.

CONTENTS

VOYAGE

Grounding

GROUNDING

I never saw the ocean as a child
but felt instead the inland tides
of morning chores and evening chores
and all the tasks that fell between
those shores — the splash of milk
from pail to strainer and the frothy rising
and the draining down inside the can.

I felt the tug of duty from a stone boat
crossing a sea of new-turned soil. A season later
grasses lured me, waving green and all together,
rooted singly, planted deep. When snow descended
I was called by sheep and cattle
and I ferried hay across the banks and barriers,
always eagerly received.

Sometimes I wondered at the town kids,
thinking they must drift like snowflakes,
light and free, without the careful watch
of time and weather. They must feel loose as seeds
caught in a summer wind,
without the heaving patch of earth
that anchored me.

I TASTE THE GREEN

I taste the green of Daddy's John Deere tractor,
the tang of mustard yellow trim,
the contours of a seat worn paintless,
the iron throne that carries him across a fresh-plowed field
at sunset. And I stretch to feel
the thudding flywheel, thumping engine,
huge work-horse tires chewing the loamy soil.
I touch the tractor's distant drumming,
striking louder, stronger on the edge of twilight,
and I hear my smile as he rides in.

WATER GIRL

It has some drawbacks, being six years old —
a girl besides. I'm way too small
for all the big, important harvest work
and will be sent on pint-sized errands
like toting water to the men
on shocking days.

My short legs will be scratched to bleeding
by my trek across the fresh-cut field
but I push on, encouraged by my father's wave
then by his smiling eyes as I come near
the hoisting of that jug against his sun-parched lips
the thirsty gulping, gulping, and his careful leaving
of one quenching swallow
for his water girl.

Halfway toward home I might find refuge in a shock of oats.
With folded limbs I barely fit inside that space.
There I'll be cradled, safe and quiet
in a secret place. Who could imagine
that I might be curled inside those cooling walls?
No one will search or call —
they all have pressing chores and have forgotten me —
but I am satisfied to drift awhile
in a small straw boat
upon the stubbled sea.

NEW KITTENS

By summer's end they will be shrieking predators
or bony beggars,
impossible to catch and tough to love.
Before snow flies they should be stalking rodents in the granary,
tripping us as we pour frothy pails of milk into the strainer
or hunching open-mouthed beneath distended teats.

But maybe not.
One could be rat-poisoned by then,
one stomped by an impatient hoof,
another flattened by four stomachs
housed in one giant beast.
And there's the stock tank
where whole litters have been sacked and tied
for gasping death.

For now the haymow is alive
with miracles. I'll climb up once —
or maybe twice — and be amazed
by so much life in one sweet nest of timothy.

One by one I'll weigh them on my palm —
the gray, the black, the tabby —
press lips and nose against the downy fur,
finger the featherlight bones.

Three visits could result in love;
I won't risk that.
But I can listen at the hay chute
for a week or two
and hear their mewling
under timber skies.

JEANNIE OF BALSAM ACRES

Mama was right — a mutt might do as well, our father laughed,
but I'm a fool and I paid fifty dollars for this pup —
a border collie, bred to work with sheep and cattle.
She's registered, you see, like royalty.
Her name is Jeannie —
Jeannie of Balsam Acres.

She earned her price and lived up to that lofty name
for three grand years. With grace and diligence
she guided straying ewes and lagging lambs to greener grasses,
herding, coaxing, scolding, chasing,
circling back for adoration.

Three sunburned shepherds dressed in calico
fanned her with balsam branches,
combed burrs and thistles from her snowy ruff,
sang praises, necklaced her
with braided clover.

A highborn beauty needed more than docile sheep and easy love.
She nipped the hocks of fleeing pickup trucks on County Y
until one August day a jagged fender caught her throat
and laid it bare. Her life drained quickly, thick and red
upon the blacktopped road.

Our father dug a burial vault beyond the lilac hedge
where we positioned Jeannie's legs
for everlasting chase,
then with our forearms rolled the dark earth down
until our collie's coat had vanished
like a sun.

FUNERAL GAMES

Leanne died late in March, the year my twin and I turned eight.
She lay cocooned in silk, there in the farmhouse parlor where we three
played hide and seek on rainy days, huddling wordlessly
behind couches and cupboards, collecting dustballs, bruising knees.
Touch your cousin, say good-bye, our mother whispered
but I couldn't make my fingers reach that far —
already she was galaxies away, hard as a distant star.

She was not hiding in that husk that barely looked like her —
that much I knew. Her living face
would not have come so clean, those perfect curls would be undone.
She would have worn a rumpled jersey, baggy overalls,
never agreed to ruffled organdy the color of a sun-washed sky.
She'd go with dirt-stained knuckles, too,
and grubby fingernails, the way we all came up
from playing funeral games, planting dead sparrows,
chipmunks, other small cadavers in the wormy earth, giggling,
singing their souls to heaven with promises of glorious rebirth.

Leanne had flown there alone, for keeps —
no warning, no permission — leaving her barn boots on the stoop,
her matted mittens dangling down from empty sleeves,
toys scattered, porch swing pumping in the breeze.

At suppertime our parents talked of planting.
Tomorrow I'll start plowing the west forty —
corn should thrive back there, our father said.
Mama nodded. *That north field is so depleted —*
better seed it with alfalfa, don't you think?
My twin and I laid summer plans that night as we undressed for bed.
We wouldn't do those silly funerals anymore.
We're eight years old, for heaven's sake.
We ought to help more, I agree.
Take charge of mowing lawn —
Wash dishes every day — and weed the garden —
Willingly.

NORTHERN LIGHTS

One frosty night
I lingered near the barn beside my father
when our evening chores were through.

The northern lights washed back and forth across the sky
licking the galaxies
with milk and fire.

You have to look up now and then
to know how small you are
was all he said.

I whispered *yes*
but saw a truth quite opposite.
I gripped the Dipper in my mittened hand
and felt quite satisfied to know
his calloused finger could erase the bright North Star.

IN THE HOLLOW

Out on the eastern fringe of our L-shaped farm
beyond the hinge of fertile fields and pastures
lies a lunar landscape pocked by a dozen craters,
each one smooth and circular
and large enough to hold a lid of stars.

Our father guesses that these kettles were scooped out
several million years ago by ice and boulders
crawling the frozen earth. He is impressed
and strangely satisfied by rugged places
that resist a plow.

Wild columbine and black-eyed-Susan
thrive in the summer silence of those hollows.
In the winter months deep drifts of snow
cast purple-fingered shadows that can clutch a child,
lay her inside that bowl and leave her mesmerized,
riding the clouds that inch across the glacial skies.

Splicing the Rope

SPLICING THE ROPE

There would be little rest for any crewman
on a 1950's haying day,
little respite from the growling tractors, hissing heat,
blue dust of stem and leaf baled tight,
the bite of twinestring,
sharp and throbbing through thick leather gloves.

My father liked to work the mow,
shielded from engines, shouting men and grinding sun.
He smiled to see the iron spider crawl its web
with eight dense bales gripped fast in its forked legs —
up, up —
enjoyed the twisting, groaning of the rope,
the hesitation of a swiveling cargo at the open peak,
the quaking pulley and the running in across a fast, straight track —
Whoa! Trip 'er! — the resulting din,
the bouncing bricks of baked alfalfa at his feet.

The mow man didn't seem to mind
hefting those heavy bales, straining to keep the pace,
smoothing the cliffs and caverns of his dim domain.
He also called the halt, perhaps too joyfully,
each time the hayrope frayed or broke,
for he could sit then and create a great, long splice.
He made fine craft of it, a braid so perfect
that it took on meaning of its own.
Quite lost in this, he worked with naked, nimble fingers
and an artist's attitude, until a crewman called
My gawd, what's going on up there?
We're ready with another load!

Finished or not, he had to let his masterpiece go down
to meet the test.
It came up strong and steady, bearing the weight,
again,
again,
again.

THRESHING DAY

Early each autumn a gigantic monster named McCormick-Deering
crawled up our driveway, pulled by a growling green John Deere.
Grain spout, straw blower pipe, feed apron had been folded for the ride,
belts rolled and stored inside its empty belly. Even in sleep,
it crushed small stones beneath its iron feet.

Unfolding and awakening with furious appetite,
the dinosaur brought chomping, wheezing, banging climax
to a season of relentless work and worry. A crew of seven sweaty men
dismantled golden shocks, hauled bundles from the sun-baked field,
and pitched them toward the gaping maw.
The creature spit back polished oats; its bowels thundered
as they blew out sweet clean straw.

September 1953, my brother Teddy — eight years old — climbed topside,
rode there like a king trembling with power. He reigned for minutes only,
soon dethroned by angry shouts and shaking fists.
Daddy and his neighbor held a spongy stance atop the bundle wagon,
one misstep from frightful jaws and hacking teeth.
They laughed and yelled above the din, not caring
that they perched so near the end of life.
Daddy jumped down, hauled himself beneath the drive belt
for a quick inspection as it squealed and whined, a deadly bandsaw,
inches from his head. *Belt started slipping! Shut 'er down for now —*
It's time to eat!

They gathered in, mopping red necks and brows with their bandannas,
spilling chaff from cuffs and pockets.
Now that's a damned fine crop, wouldn't you say?
You betcha! Nearly ninety bushels to the acre!
Mama hurried from the stove with mashed potatoes, steaming stew.
I followed after with the rhubarb pie and ice cream, strangely shy,
silenced this day by scenes of glory and disaster.

SHEARING TIME

Each spring at shearing time I perched for hours on the gate
and watched my father strip the weight from winter-weary sheep.
His clippers traveled like a plow, rolling back great banks of snowy wool,
enormous drifts that finally crested and let loose
in one great avalanche upon the canvas floor.

It was a graceful sculpting, starting at the brisket, moving slowly
over the left shoulder, head, right shoulder, down the back and rump,
the flanks, the rear. The ewes were straddled all the while,
shifted deftly into stunning postures. Once released,
they struggled up and tripped away, surprised, light-footed, free.

My father rolled and tied and weighed each fleece
and stuffed it down into a burlap sack, smiling with the satisfaction
that a healthy crop of wool could bring. He offered me
his softened hand; I held the palm against my face.
It smelled of love and lanolin and spring.

BUMMERS

We called them bummers —
what a careless name for orphaned lambs
that loved us frantically with jewel-blue eyes,
ecstatic tails, fierce bleating.

We offered nourishment, six, seven times a day,
from root-beer bottles fitted out with long black nipples
held to the bottlenecks with firm, two-fisted grips.
The lambs sucked life and gave back cleft-lip smiles.
Sometimes they yanked the nipples free when our attention slacked,
splashing cow's milk over hands and feet,
feeding the quack and clover.

Our bummers thrived but never blended fully with the flock,
always scrambling to the fence
whenever they heard high-pitched laughter or girl-mother voices.
They would be ours, bonded like wool to skin
long after we had anything to give,
long after they had gone to grass.

WINTER BLEATING

The long, deep season looms
like a fast train
steaming in on icy rails.

Then suddenly I am aboard,
riding
toward a treacherous tunnel.

I know too well what waits within:
reluctant risings,
tardy sun,
school bus journeys dark to dark,
silent suppers,
parents tired beyond speech
from wrestling hay bales to a flock of sheep,
pitching frozen silage to the bawling cattle,
chipping ice from water cups,
scooping the gutters clean.

Dramatic work, dramatic play.
I will have towering drifts to climb,
snowmen to build and decorate,
a slick toboggan to be crashed against the gray blue skies,
and lullabies from woolly animals
who'll keep close company inside their shed.

Some nights their bleating will disturb instead.
Winter is not a game.
Can't you do more to help?
Can't you do more?

NOURISHMENT

I often wondered at the basic difference
between sheep and cattle. Mama was partial to the cows.
Once acquainted with an udder — each was as different as a face —
she could drain it efficiently with caring movements
that resembled love.

More likely it was economics. Managed well,
cows could be counted on the year around, like fine machines,
for turning grass and corn and oats to milk and cheese and butter
and a rich manure that fueled the earth.

Mama stood awhile when she poured milk into the strainer,
heard it rain down through the sieve, inside the hollow can.
She relished, too, serving a tasty roast or stew
made from the butchered culls that had no more to give.

Our father favored sheep, although they paid off only twice a year —
wool in the month of May, a load of fattened lambs each fall,
and both depended on capricious markets.
Too much like gambling, Mama said. *Cows are your daily bread —
this is dairy country. He'll see that soon enough.*

He never did.
We saw him work in bursts of pride and passion every spring,
assisting risky births, swaddling chilled lambs in his jacket,
grafting rejected twins or orphans to the care of foster ewes,
digging stillborns down beneath the roots of clover.
And at shearing time we heard him singing in the shed all day,
at sundown watched him weigh and bundle up the snowy fleece.

We never ate a single lamb or barren ewe. I wonder why
no one suggested some variety from stringy beef.
Was it the plaintive bleating of the flock on summer nights?
Their winter lullabies? Their glowing eyes or trusting attitudes?
Some Biblical association? No, we were shallow Christians
and had greedy appetites. I think we sensed a higher nourishment
and had to keep our silence for the shepherd, not the sheep.

THE COWS ARE OUT

Our mother's agitated voice
rides on the dawn, at milking time:
Quick, kids — we need your help! The cows are out!

We stagger up from patchwork sleep,
pull on stiff overalls and shirts and shoes,
fly down to meet the dreaded task.
The cause is clear — a skittish heifer
stormed the new electric fence, crashed through.
Now, spiked with energy,
she leads a dozen bawling sisters
on a wild tour of Mama's garden.

Freedom confounds them.
They churn excitedly across the rows,
trampling the cabbages, bell peppers, tall tomatoes,
ripping pea vines,
bringing the cornstalks down.

My sisters and I know our moves:
arms splayed like scarecrows, we fan out,
we sing and shout,
press toward the barnyard gate, surround,
surround. Our mother coaxes and cajoles —
come, boss, come boss —
while Daddy's wired curses spook the cattle
and move kids to prayer —
please, God, please help us get them in.
The Holsteins stall and shift and shy,
go off ten maddened ways, then somehow
gain some sense and stumble home.

Weak-kneed, we climb the stairs to bed,
sink down to sleep,
dampened by sweat and dew
and breath of cows,
charged with electric dreams.

GRACE

Grim duty took me to the barn
each night at choring time.
I trailed behind my father whose reluctant gait
was joyless as my own.

My little sister — only five —
relished that humid, heaving place.
A chord of perfume — briny mix of cow manure,
raw milk, corn silage, moldy hay and steaming piss —
drew her inside.

There she amused herself with risky games —
cat chasing, rope swinging, hay-hole diving,
to name just a few. One night she threw herself
into a nest of broken bales and came up
marked by bloody stripes on either side
of her small neck.

Look, Daddy! Here's that old pitchfork you lost!
I landed right between the tines!
He didn't hear at first, good ear and forehead
pressed into his work. She called again —
Look, Daddy!
Perfect landing!

He left milkers surging on empty udders
and rocked his saved child there in the hay,
back and forth, back and forth.
And when I glimpsed his face in that dim manger;
it looked strangely bright, washed bare
by gratitude and grace.

MOVING UP

It wrenched the world, that five mile move from Balsam Lake to Milltown.
The new farm was slightly smaller — only a hundred acres —
but nearly all of that was under plow, flat, fertile, clean.
No stone boats would go sailing there.
There were no lowland sloughs, no errant trees or lazy lakes to work around.
One winter sledding hill to please the kids, and that was all —
the rest was pasture land or pure production.

Yes, we were moving up in 1953, that much was clear.
The barn was big enough for forty cattle, two brick silos towering near.
The house was square and sturdy, four big bedrooms up, another down.
A telephone, bathroom and running water for the family.
Nearly an even trade — all this exchanged for swamps and hills and hollows,
ponds and creeks and wasted forest land, fit only for the birds
and squirrels and ducks and deer.

Our father walked the ground that stretched before him like a promise,
head down, studying the soil.
Later I guessed he wasn't doing that at all. He'd only wandered there
to contemplate his losses, seeing prospects of unbroken toil,
drought of spirit, flat despair.

BALSAM BEACH

Some summer days, with hay half-cocked
and field corn struggling up in quacky rows
my father had to swim at Balsam Beach.

You're going NOW? My mother asked,
This afternoon? With hay cut and exposed to stormy weather?
There was no sense to it, of course. If anything
the pull of Balsam Beach was stronger when the clouds collided,
adding risk to devilish demands on time and temper.

Minutes later but a world away
I heard the town boys laughing at his farmer's tan —
veiny blue-white legs, brown forearms, leathered face
and sunburned V-neck pointing toward a milky chest —
all marks of bondage to the land.

I watched my father from the shallows as he plunged
into the purging cold, plowed to the raft and clamored up,
poised his lean body, drilled it down
into the furrowed lake.

Sometimes he hurled himself to shore with flywheel arms,
stalled in the sand and sputtered like a spent machine.
Sometimes he filled his lungs and drifted like a buoyant cross,
arms splayed, sky resting on his face.
And either way I witnessed
resurrection.

Whipped Cream on Sunday

WHIPPED CREAM ON SUNDAY

One Sunday morning — 1952, I think, for I was nine —
our trucker dropped a helpful hint to Mama
as he hoisted milk cans from the cooling tank.
He'd worked at Land-O-Lakes for sixteen years,
he said, and never once in all that time
had they checked butterfat content on Sundays.
Good chance, once every week, to skim some cream,
whip up a treat to feed the family.

Each Sabbath after that, for years to come,
I was allowed to raid the cans
before I went to church and Sunday School.
I scooped rich clots out of those silver throats,
laid bare the necks of blue-white milk,
then hammered down the heavy lids.
They pealed like bells.

Remorseless, I sang morning praises
to a jealous God. At noon
I glorified the rice, Jello and apple pie
with clouds of cream, sweetened by greed,
whipped high for sinful appetites.

SUNDAY DRIVE

The Sunday drive was an indulgence, verging on recklessness,
unplanned. It just happened now and then, decades ago
on summer Sunday afternoons,
beginning with Daddy's quiet, almost shy suggestion
that we might go out driving —
to compare the neighbors' crops, you know.

That was the stated reason
but we often traveled way beyond our section,
through a town or two, or even three.
We might expend two precious hours and a tank of gasoline,
risk puncturing thin tires on coarse gravel roads,
take chances with small rocks that shattered windshields in a heartbeat,
unsettling incidents that could not be controlled.

Mama, Daddy, all five kids piled into the DeSoto,
and we headed out, contained in our own free-wheeling world.
Probably we'd drive right by an uncle's farm — not even stop or wave —
and risk the possibility that he might spot our vehicle
and later question our strange liberty.

There were some crop reviews along the way,
conducted by our mother who craved purpose.
That corn of Einer Anderson's is awfully late ...
Jack Nelson seeded oats there three years running ...
wouldn't you think he'd want to give that ground a break,
maybe rotate to alfalfa?
That stand of timothy looks mighty thin, if you ask me.

No one was asking her, of course.
We didn't care about lush stands of corn and oats and hay —
not on this day when we were ranging in the wider world.
The fields and farmsteads looked so transient flying by,
so poorly founded in the landscape — surely not strong or deep enough
to claim a person's whole long life,

to swallow generations of a family's time and energy and caring.
Yet I knew they did;
they did.

It could be quite disturbing — such a far-flung tour,
lacking in reason and clear destination.
One had to realize that the world could be capricious
with its tricks and chances, accidents of death and birth, hard choices
like commitment to a place, or no commitment — rootlessness —
and all the wild-eyed freedom that might bring.
If Daddy stopped in town for root beer
or a round of ice cream — *Big double-deckers, please!* —
it was more than a happy splurge.
It was an anchoring, a soothing pause
that readied us for going home again.

LONG– LONG– SHORT– LONG

Our farmhouse telephone looked like a creature
born of wood and wire.
Squareheaded, it was fitted out with bulging silver eyes,
a long black beak connected to a flaring mouth,
a pair of mismatched ears —
cylindrical receiver dangling down the left side,
short metal crank protruding on the right.

It shrilled all day from its position on the kitchen wall,
a different ring for every family on the party line,
and there were twelve of them;
we knew them all.
LONG-LONG-SHORT-LONG —
that brought four daughters running hopefully.
The calls were usually for Mama,
who fluffed her hair out with a nervous hand,
tucked in her blouse and smiled
as if her friends could spy right through the snout.

LAUNDRY, 1954

It would be tackled on a Saturday
when all four daughters were at home to help.
Mama ran the job, rewarding speed and sunny dispositions
with sweet smelling chores like pegging clothes out on the line,
or gathering in.

That wasn't me.
I usually sorted dirties in great heaps upon the kitchen floor,
never mastering the complex rules concerning weight of fabric,
color, odor, depth of dirt. *Towels go in this stack,*Mama said,
that is unless they're red or purple — those make a separate load —
they won't be colorfast. Sheets, pillowcases here,
school clothing there, except for underwear.
Check crotches carefully — the stained ones get a special soak and scrub.
Now start that tub of whites — no, not those smelly shirts —
they'll wait till near the end. And barn pants, overalls, go last.

The sorting, soaping, dashing, wringing, bluing,
rinsing, wringing, rinsing, wringing again,
the hanging, drying, taking down consumed our day.
We finally saw the last foul load of overalls go in —
Oshkosh B'Gosh went churning in a gray-blue soup
garnished with straw.
They crawled up through the wringer, somewhat cleaner,
though I wondered how. Their buckles caught between the rollers,
made them gasp and stall and fly apart.
An easy fix, said Mama, to my great dismay.

The washer drained out slowly, clogged by a silty mix of soil,
chaff, manure and broken buttons, stones and screws
and God-knows-what-men-put-in-their-cuffs-and-pockets.
We made pancakes for supper, too weary for the usual roast or stew.
That was some job we did today! chirped Mama.
Don't you feel good?
We rolled our eyes and sighed, *Sure do.*

PICKLES

A kid could grow up hating pickles
after spending priceless days bent over itchy vines.
But dill spears lined up straight as captured soldiers
in a mason jar, or bread-and-butters in sweet onion brine
bear no resemblance to the spiny fruit that pierces gloved hands,
stains them bright green, cramps legs and backs,
steals lazy afternoons.

It's war, of course. And you will win —
mere pickles can't prevail for long.
You can forgive a gherkin in a jar for hiding while it had a chance,
camouflaged beneath broad leaves, hoping
you'd pass on by repeatedly so it could gain some size,
planning its ambush as a jumbo ghost, mushy and pale,
not worth a squat.

Few come to that. Relentlessly you roust them out —
the small crisp cukes so highly prized.
Left and right you snatch them from their sprawling ranks,
toss them inside your sack. And still those vines
send out their tendrils in the August heat, wave yellow blooms
like victory flags until, quite suddenly, they weaken and retreat
like a spent summer.

CHRISTMAS QUESTIONS

Through every season
a farm kid witnesses the core events,
studies the major mysteries
of bloody birth
and bloated death
and heated coupling.

Enough to ponder.
Then winter comes down white and hushed,
bringing a plate of puzzles
like Jack Frost,
the Virgin Birth
and reindeer paws and Santa Claus.

Discerning kids might want to ask:
How does a North Pole Santa
driving a sleigh — eight reindeer too —
manage to leave a bulging burlap sack
on the back stoop,
undetected,
just as a father lumbers in,
just as the evening chores are through?

Why does the sack smell like ground oats?
Why is it marked *Midland Co-Op*?
And why do the gifts come packaged
in the same old wraps and ribbons,
smoothed by a mother's careful hand,
stored and recycled, year to year?

They hold their questions.
Even a first grade child can see the happy humbug
in this Christmas game,
the simple fraud,
sweet trickery.

CUTTING UP

My twin and I were handy with our mother's scissors at an early age.
We chopped each other's hair for practice, and snipped paper dolls
with fancy wardrobes from the mail order catalog.

By 1952, when we turned nine, we had advanced to bigger things —
our own ball gowns and ballet costumes
fashioned from Mama's stash of yardgoods
or from cast-off clothing, hand-me-downs awaiting second lives.

One rainy day we searched her closet,
came across a dusty-rose crepe dress abandoned there
way in the back, a droopy thing we'd never seen her wear.
We snatched it out. *Chenille sleeves!* Susie laughed,
clipping the ditches of that furrowed fabric,
making fuzzy ribbons that might serve as trim.
The skirt is long and full — we could make tu-tu's out of that! I grinned.

We cut and stitched all afternoon, then dressed and danced out to the garden
like two wild roses infested with small worms of pink chenille.
Mama straightened up from her cucumber vines,
rubbed her forehead with a tired sigh, then stared.
My wedding dress! she gasped.
We stood there, rooted by guilt and shame,
astonished by her sudden tears.

DANCING THE COWS HOME

My early years were lush with play and possibilities.
Expanding choices dazzled me each day. I could become
an opera star in Rome, the queen of Hollywood,
a circus acrobat, a dancer in the French ballet.

I leaned toward dance. I pirouetted in the pasture
when I fetched the cattle home. The stupid things
went lumbering along, quite unimpressed by arabesques,
tall leaps and twirls. Their slow eyes didn't see
my baggy denims had been traded in for silk chiffon,
my muddy saddle shoes were gone —
I wore pink slippers on my flying feet.

The Holsteins shook their heavy heads, bawled loudly,
raised bony tails and splashed their cowpies down
in front of me, fresh insults that disdained my far-flung plans,
my budding grace and joyful artistry.

I'd like to blame those sluggish brutes for my diminished dreams.
Yes, that was it — those cows conspired to keep me homebound,
safe and small. As childhood waned so did my wild energy.
I saw myself through bovine eyes,
a clumsy farm girl with a clutch of fantasies.
I saw the world was fenced and ordered after all.

SKATING NEAR THE BARN

A frozen pond formed in the winter, near the barn
where Daddy emptied pails full of gray-green water with a reckless fling
when he had finished swabbing Holsteins' udders.

Here I went sailing in the black, long-bladed hockey skates
saved from his high school days.
My ankles wobbled in the outsized gear
that I had padded with four pairs of woolen socks
and lashed against my skinny calves with loops of baling twine.

Round and around I turned,
rehearsing spins and circles on that tiny rink,
accompanied by mooing cows and surging milk machines.

The cold white stars spotlighted me
and moonbeams followed every awkward move I made.
But I was cheered by yellow light
that glowed behind each quartered window frame,
warmed by the faith and fortitude within that pulsing place,
fueled by an energy I could not name.

CIRCLE SKIRT

My thirteenth birthday gift was grand:
the circle skirt I had been coveting
from Sears and Roebuck's catalog.
It came by Parcel Post, packaged in cellophane —
a flaring field of poplin daisies that invited me
to leap and whirl till I was dizzy with my own blooming.

Within a season I had spun out of childhood,
landing in a place I vaguely recognized by moon-sized aching
and a patch of bloodied flowers on my skirt
as big as Jupiter. Time cycled seamlessly

there was no fuss, no ritual dancing,
only some Kotex planted in my bureau drawer
and Mama's helpful hints: this thing would keep on happening
for forty years, as regular as laundry.
Try Oxydol and ice cold water on that stain —
that ought to lift it free.

It didn't, though. A stubborn pink bouquet
clung to the fabric, marking that day,
that first of many circling woman-days,
indelibly.

THE COFFEE TRAIN

Each Tuesday afternoon, all through my fourteenth winter
I rode the Soo Line coffee train, leaving at 3:09 P.M. from Milltown depot.
I sat on plush maroon, traveling north five miles to the town of Luck
for piano lessons. And in waning light — lavender, blue —
the southbound train brought me back home
with aging women, coffeed up, filled to the brim with local news.

Their chatter warmed me. I might also hear
harsh conversation from a city pair, well dressed, well traveled,
bored by the miles behind them, miles to go.
They often napped, these city folks, or scanned their papers
sipping coffee, talking of places with impressive names —
Duluth, Chicago. What they didn't do
was look for windswept sculpture in the open fields,
admire the dairy barns — blood-red against the snow —
brick silos, slatted corncribs bulging with golden cobs,
tidy white houses, deep-eaved, hung with icicles, graced by green pines.
They also missed the hunkering flocks of sheep, the Holsteins —
hides like Mercator maps, black shapes on white —
held tight in barnyard worlds.

Sometimes the coffee talk was so unsettling.
> *I couldn't stand this quiet life, could you? Nothing to do...*
> *no shops, no restaurants, no concerts, cultured company...*
> *Do you think every tiny village has a name?*
> *Of course it does — see there — we're coming into LUCK.*
> *Sounds like a joke. I think I'd die in such a place.*

The train rolled past a graveyard, drifted deep,
and I considered country lives played out, pianissimo,
in this uncelebrated space. Inside my head
I played Bach's Minuet in G, again, again,
to clear the words away, but they were thumping there,
laying a track that I would have to travel on another day.

Voyage

OLAVA'S GARDEN

When I was small I gave the name Olava
to a bush in Grandma's garden that bowed low with lacy blooms.
Hydrangea, probably. I later learned
Olava was my Grandma's name. A logical confusion
since she, too, was rooted in the garden
and flowers seemed to be the only thing that made her smile.

Well, so did I, occasionally, with girlish chatter
when I helped her groom the dahlias, cosmos, primrose, peonies,
laughing pansies bounding up from tidy beds.
I hung close by and watched her weave blue morning glories
through the trellis and stake hollyhocks — shell pink, magenta —
near the kitchen door.

I heard her humming as she weeded, watered,
trimmed and trained all summer long
and had to wonder why she never brought a single blossom in.

Her life inside the farmhouse looked so stooped and cheerless
and her shoulders arched like heavy bowers on too slight a frame,
weighted by time at breadboards, washtubs, mixing bowls.
The work was less these days, but she was well bent down
and any straightening might break her like a brittle stem,
just like a splash of flowers on the table could be too unnerving
in this quiet time, with children grown and gone.

Uff-da! she said, a dozen times each day,
a mild Norwegian curse at minor mishaps,
small surprises, good and bad alike.
Oh, shit! That was her sharp American complaint
when Grandpa spat tobacco or tracked mud and cow manure
across a fresh-scrubbed floor.

Oh, shit! each time he ate a hurried meal,
pushed back his chair and took his leave

without a thank-you or a sweet good-bye.
And she would shuffle, then, table to dishpan,
in the tired ritual of some sixty years of parched togetherness with him.

Nine children reared and scattered like a pod of seeds,
only some fleeting visits now and then,
and curious grand-kids blowing in.
Uff-da to that.

She smiled at me, or at the Shasta daisies that rose up between us,
yet she never hugged me, never once in all those years,
just like she never gathered in her blooms.

Olava died at ninety-one, when I was twenty-three. I didn't cry
but grieved my losses as she might have done.
Oh, shit. Who's going to bed those roses for the winter?
Who's going to weave those wild vines into their frames each spring?
Trim errant stalks as summer wanes?
Stake up the tipping hollyhocks?

INVENTORY

At ninety-three, Aunt Margaret is still too vital,
too connected, to let loose her valuables.
But she agrees to take an inventory,
winnow, label, store, or plan to give away.
Some day.

She frets about a Plymouth hatchback
she no longer drives. Some crystal bowls.
A stereo system and a stack of record albums
that she purchased thirty years ago with hard-earned cash.
And there's her manual Smith-Corona —
Such a fine machine —
someone should have the use of it.
I don't have heart to say it's all computers now
and I suspect she'll have to pay to have it carted off.
Let's start with small stuff, I suggest.

She nods. We empty boxes, bureau drawers
filled with decades of correspondence,
some of it dull, clogged with the chaff of self-defense,
more of it pithy, real, small private truths
of a specific place, polished by time. We read and laugh
and weep and reminisce, discarding little in three days —
certainly none of brother Raymond's formal tomes
penned back in 1944, the year
he filled his pockets up with stones and waded deep
into the Apple River and sank down to silence.
She won't surrender anything he wrote,
a single picture of his smiling face.

Aunt Margaret cherishes the melancholy notes
from 'Mama', penciled in 1923, still sharp with worry,
bleak with loss and longing for a first-born daughter
who must have a city life.

She sorts through dozens of sweet notes
from the city man who called her Sunshine,
married her, moved her to southern California.
She saves each newsy letter from folks back home —
they're precious history, after all, filled with particulars —
dry, dusty fields, thin crops of hay and oats
and withered corn, stiff winds, deep snows,
milk fever laying low the herd,
fat, healthy hens, but what a dismal price for eggs!
Depression men, hunched in despair, riding the rails,
the wireless, the REA, the War To End All Wars —
the black and white of it, all fresh, all there,
bold on the page.

The early letters from her son in Viet Nam
are written tall, loopy with patriotic pride. Later
his hand is cramped and small. News straggles home,
vague and detached. He'll come back, too,
looking like that.
The gentle-hearted ought to be deferred!
she cries. She treasures every image
of his laughing eyes, each souvenir of innocence —
the Boy Scout badges, school reports
and home made valentines.

Some day these keepsakes will be all that's left,
Aunt Margaret sighs, arranging photographs
in careful order, sepia tones to living color.
She ties the parcels of her own chronology
with salvaged string, all to be boxed and catalogued
and stored again. The stack looks higher than before.
I know I'm too attached, she says, apologetically,
I can't let go of anything, not yet.
Maybe tomorrow...

GLUTTON WORMSALL

Decades ago I shared five minutes with a robin
by the name of Glutton Wormsall.
My little brother gave that name
to an abandoned bird he found
cold on the ground, beneath the lilacs.
> *Oh, look! He's breathing!*

I squatted down and saw the nestling's open maw
stretched wide enough to swallow its own head,
take in a world of worms, convert them
into feathers, flight and song.
I saw the small dark heart, fine web of veins
pumping beneath transparent tissue,
stretching for life so newly given, so nearly gone.

Bright robin eyes stared into mine,
drew me inside that throbbing sack of skin.
We sucked, together, at the thinning pulse of air
and knew how weak our live connection
to the blinking earth
and how capricious the unplugging.

I twisted free from that thin strand of energy
just as my brother offered up a wriggling worm.
The bird's beak closed,
its head went loose, unstrung, against a naked breast.
> *Oh, no! I came too late — he's dead!*
> *Will Glutton Wormsall go to heaven?*
> *What do you really think?*
He's there, I said.

REAL ESTATE

Today I may have done some cosmic business —
or possibly it was a simple thing
dressed up by dew and slanting light,
viewed through the magnifying lens of spring.

I didn't travel far from home today — less than a quarter mile
to an unnamed pond well ringed by trees.
There was the wood duck house my father built
and nailed to a massive oak last April, weeks before he died.
A little late, I think, for spring arrivals,
it hung vacant and unclaimed all year around.
Maybe, too, that strange decor, that wild advertising
turned potential residents away.
(The house was made from cast-off realty signs
that screamed VACATION PROPERTIES to eastbound waterfowl
and CENTURY 21 to westbound flyers.)

Today I met a fine, flamboyant duck
perched on a nearby branch, eyeing this real estate
the way a farmer cocks his head, squints at a fresh-turned field,
takes in the lay of land and nods with pride.
The duck sat firm on that low branch, as if transfixed
by recognition of a site selected once before.

I closed on him with timid steps,
awed by his regal crest, outrageous coloring and rainbow sheen.
I met his eyes and saw someone I knew beneath that grand disguise.
His steady gaze told me he planned to stay, awhile anyway,
and bless the effort of an earth-bound farmer
who had loved ducks and songbirds,
and had honored them with his crude carpentry.

This looked like home.
He'd move right in and spend the summer
here, again.
Near me.

VOYAGE

After some forty years of farming
Daddy built a sailing sloop inside an old sheep shed.
His vessel rose upon a sea of dried manure,
landlocked and huge,
the bowsprit poking through an open door.

How will he get it out?
Where will he sail? I fussed to Mama who, amazingly
was helping with the foolishness,
stitching the jib.

He'll find a way, she said.
But that boat never launched and in a year or two
squirrels nested in the hull.
A big dream gone awry, I thought.
He's still dry-docked,
still plowing, planting, pulling teats.

But there had been some kind of voyage —
I know that now.
He'd navigated risky swells,
tacked through a crippling sea of ordinary days
and come to shore.